hope
for
the
flowers

words and pictures by trina paulus

a newman book ∘ paulist press ∘ new york n.y. ∘ paramus n.j. ∘ toronto canada

Library of Congress Catalogue Number 74-179985

Published by Paulist Press
Editorial Office : 1865 Broadway, New York, N.Y. 10023
Business Office : Paramus, New Jersey 07652
Printed and bound in the United States of America

My thanks
to everyone
all over the world
who has helped me
believe in the butterfly.

This is the tale
of a caterpillar
who has trouble
becoming what
he really is.

It's like myself - like us.

love,
Trina

to the "more" of life —
the real revolution,

and to my father
who believed in it

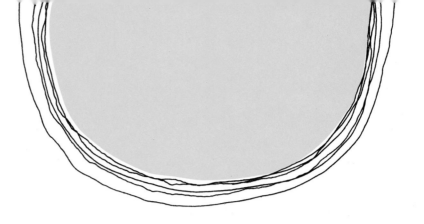

CHAPTER I

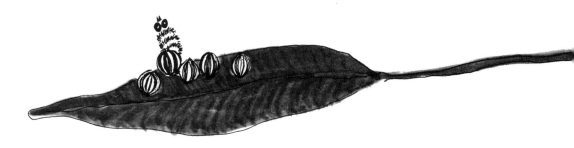

Once upon a time
a tiny striped caterpillar
burst from the egg
which had been home
for so long.

"Hello world," he said.
"It sure is bright out here in the sun."

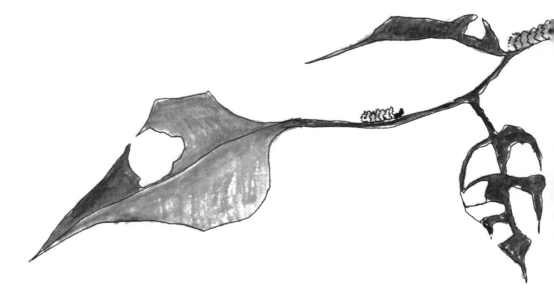

"I'm hungry," he thought
and straightway began to eat
the leaf he was born on.

And he ate another leaf... and another...

And got bigger... and bigger.

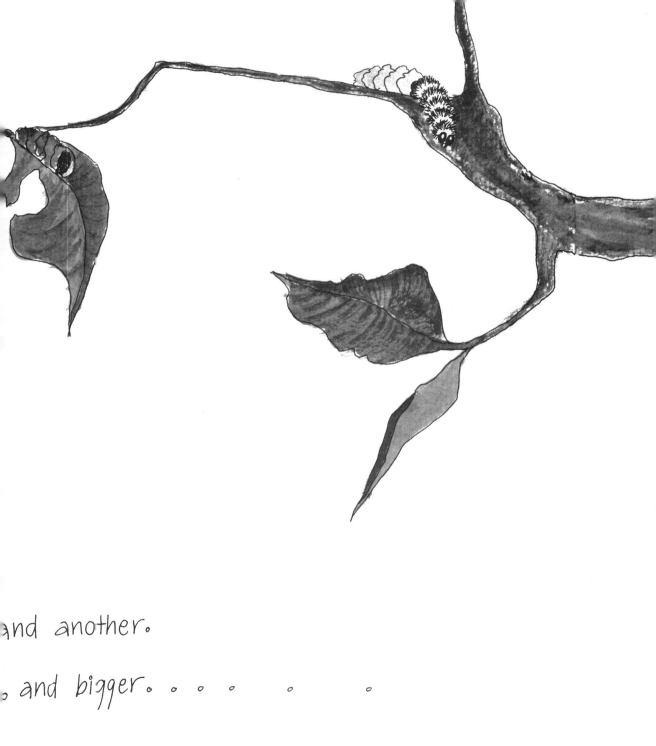

and another.

, and bigger. ° ° ° ° ° °

Until one day he stopped
eating and thought,
"There must be more to life
than just eating and
getting bigger.

"It's getting dull."

So Stripe crawled down
from the friendly tree
which had shaded and
fed him.

He was seeking more.

There were all sorts of new things
to find. Grass and dirt and holes
and tiny bugs—each fascinated him.

But nothing satisfied him.

When he came across some other crawlers like himself he was especially excited.

But they were so busy eating they had no time to talk——

just as Stripe had been.

"They don't know any more about life than I do," he sighed.

Then one day
Stripe saw some
crawlers really
crawling.

He looked around for
their goal and saw
a great column rising
high into the air.

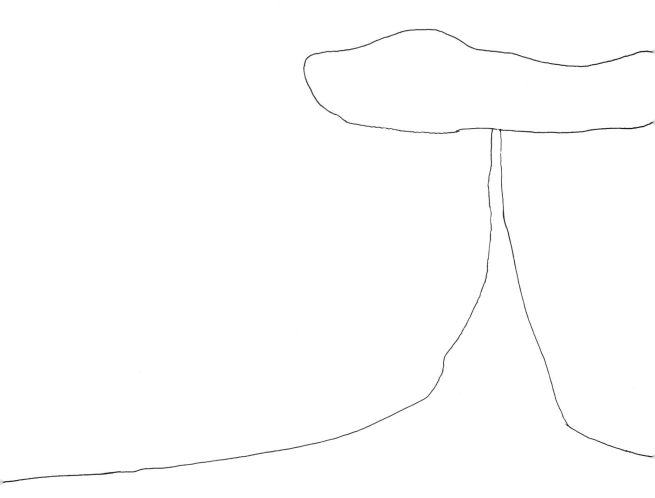

When he joined them he discovered. . . .

. . . the column was a pile of squirming,
pushing,
caterpillars—

a caterpillar pillar.

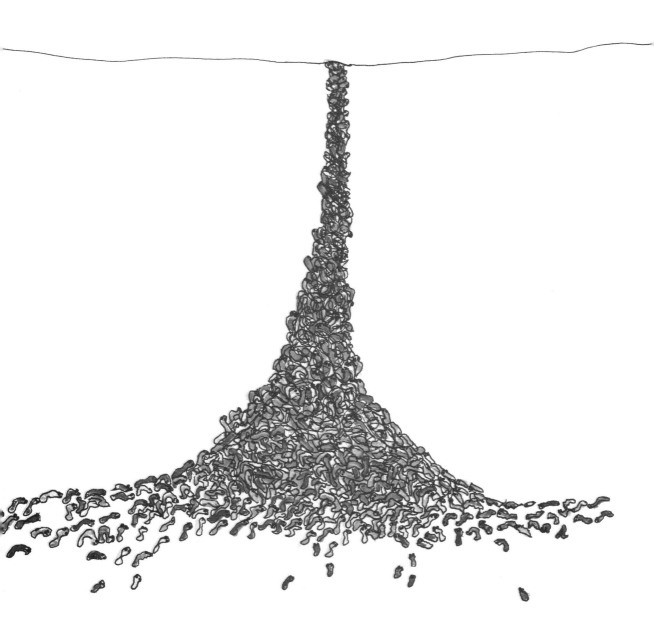

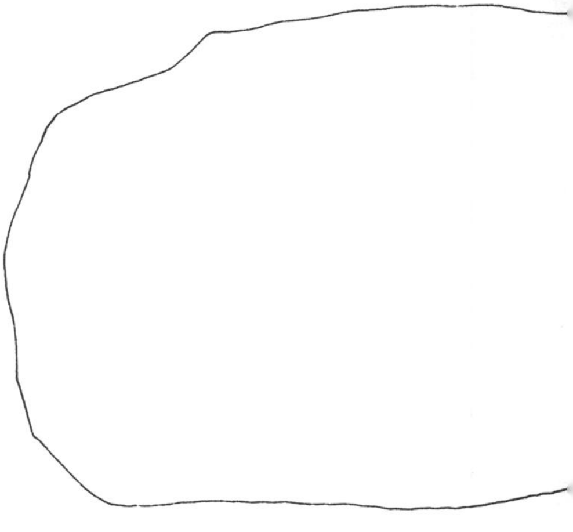

It appeared that the
caterpillars were trying
to reach the top —
but the top was so
lost in the clouds
that Stripe had no
idea what was there.

He felt new excitement —
like sap rising in the
spring.

"Maybe I'll find what
I'm looking for."

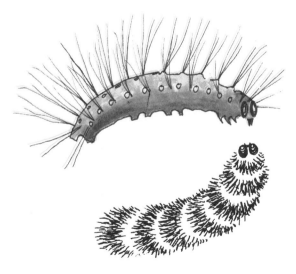

Full of agitation Stripe asked
a fellow crawler:

"Do you know what's happening?"

"I just arrived myself," said
the other. "Nobody has time
to explain; they're so busy trying
to get wherever they're going—
up there."

"But what's at the top?"
continued Stripe.

"No one knows that either but it must
be awfully good because everybody's
rushing there. Goodbye; I've no
more time!"

He plunged into the pile.

Stripe's head was bursting with the new drive. He couldn't get his thoughts together. Every second another crawler passed him and disappeared into the pillar.

"There's only one thing to do."

He pushed himself in.

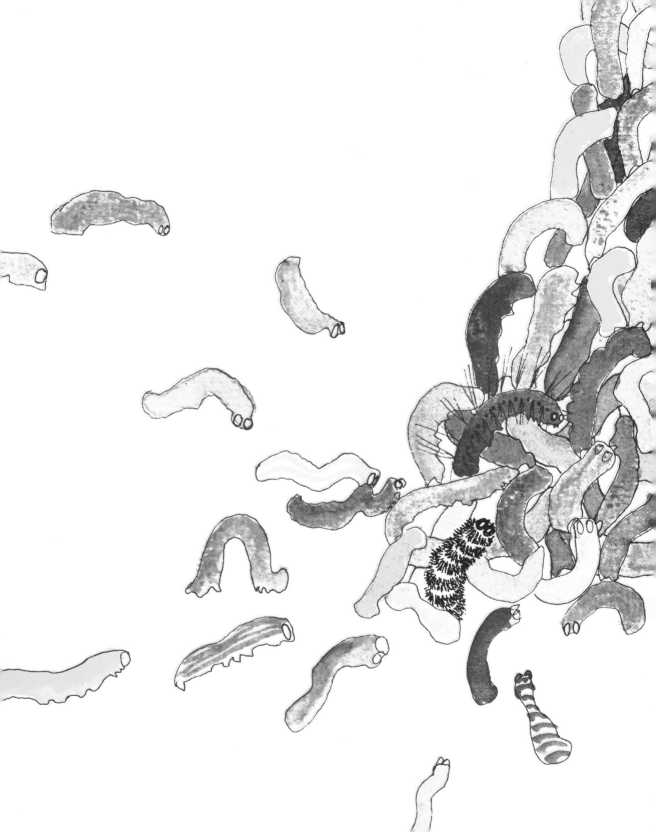

The first moments
on the pile
were a shock.

Stripe was pushed
and kicked
and stepped on
from every direction.

It was climb
or be climbed . . .

... Stripe climbed.

No more fellow caterpillars
   on Stripe's pile —
they became only threats
and obstacles which he
turned into steps and
opportunities.

This single-minded approach
really helped and Stripe
felt he was getting
much higher.

But some days it seemed
he could manage only to
keep his place. It was
especially then that an
anxious shadow nagged
inside. "What's at the
top?" it whispered.
"Where are we going?"

On one exasperated day Stripe
couldn't stand it any longer
and actually yelled back:

"I don't know, but there's
no time to think about it!"

A little yellow caterpillar he was
crawling over gasped:

"What did you say?"

"I was just talking to
myself," stripe mumbled.
"It really isn't important—
I was just wondering
where we're going?"

"You know," Yellow said, "I was wondering that myself but since there's no way to find out I decided it wasn't important." She blushed at how silly this sounded — quickly adding, "No one else seems to worry about where we're going so it must be good." But she blushed again. "How far are we from the top?"

Stripe answered gravely, "Since we're not at the bottom and not at the top we must be in the middle."

"Oh," said Yellow, and they both began climbing again.

But now
Stripe had
a new feeling.
He felt bad.

He had lost
his
singlemindedness.

"How can
I step on
someone
I've just
talked to?"

Stripe avoided Yellow as much as possible, but one day there she was, blocking the only way up.

"Well, I guess it's you or me," he said, and stepped squarely on her head.

Something in the way Yellow looked at him made him feel just awful about himself. Like: no matter what is up there — it just isn't worth it.

Stripe
crawled off
Yellow and
whispered,
" I'm sorry. "

And Yellow began to cry:

"I could stand this life hoping in what was ahead until I met you talking to yourself that day. Since then my heart just hasn't been in it — but I don't know what to do.

"I didn't know how badly I felt about this life until then. Now when you look at me so kindly, I know for sure I don't like this life. I just want to do something like crawl with you and·nibble grass."

Stripe's heart leapt inside.
Everything looked different.
The pillar made no sense at all.

"I would like that too," he whispered.

But this meant giving up the climb — a hard decision.

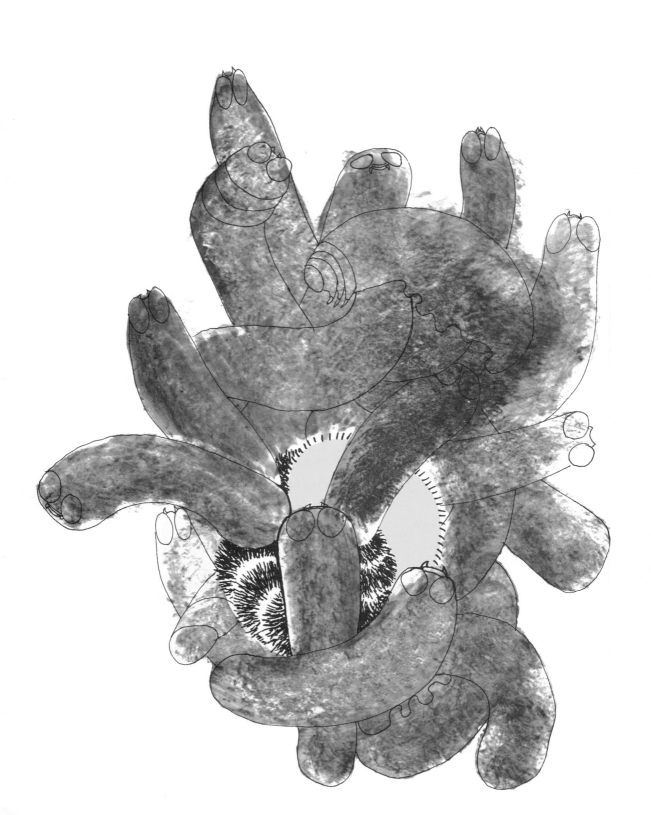

"Yellow dear, maybe we're close to the top. Maybe if we help each other we can get there quickly."

"Maybe," she said.

But they both knew this wasn't what they wanted most.

"Let's go down," Yellow said.

"Okay." And they stopped climbing.

They clung to each other as masses of caterpillars crawled over them.

The air was terrible but they were happy with each other and made a big ball so nobody could step in their eyes and stomachs.

They did nothing
at all for what
seemed a long time.

Suddenly they didn't
feel anything crawling
over them.

They unrolled and
opened their eyes.
They were at the
side of the
caterpillar pillar.

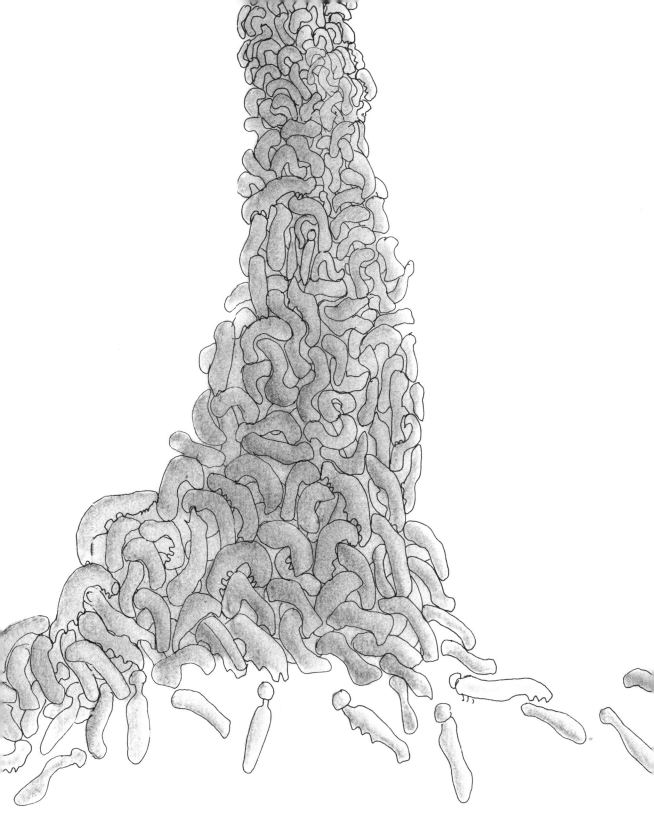

"Hi Stripe," said Yellow.

"Hi Yellow," said Stripe.

And they crawled off into
some fresh, green grass
to eat and take a nap.

Just before they fell asleep
Stripe hugged Yellow.

"Being together like this is
sure different from being
crushed in that crowd!"

"It sure is!"

She smiled and closed her eyes.

CHAPTER III

So Yellow and Stripe
romped in the grass
    and ate
    and grew fat
    and loved each other.

They were so glad
not to be fighting
everybody
every moment.

It was like heaven for a while.

But as time passed
even hugging each other
seemed a little boring.

Each knew every hair of the other.

Stripe couldn't help wondering,
"There must be still more to life."

Yellow saw how restless he was and tried to make him extra happy and comfortable. "Just think how much better this is than that awful mess we left," she said.

"But we don't know what's at the top," he answered. "Maybe we were wrong to come down. Maybe now that we've rested the two of us could make it to the top."

"Dear Stripe, please," she begged.
We have a nice home and we
love each other and that's enough.
It's so much more than all those
lonely climbers have."

She was so sure, Stripe
let her convince him.

But only for
        awhile ——

Stripe's hankering for the climbing life worsened. The pillar haunted him. He crawled there regularly, looking up and wondering.

But the top remained clouded.

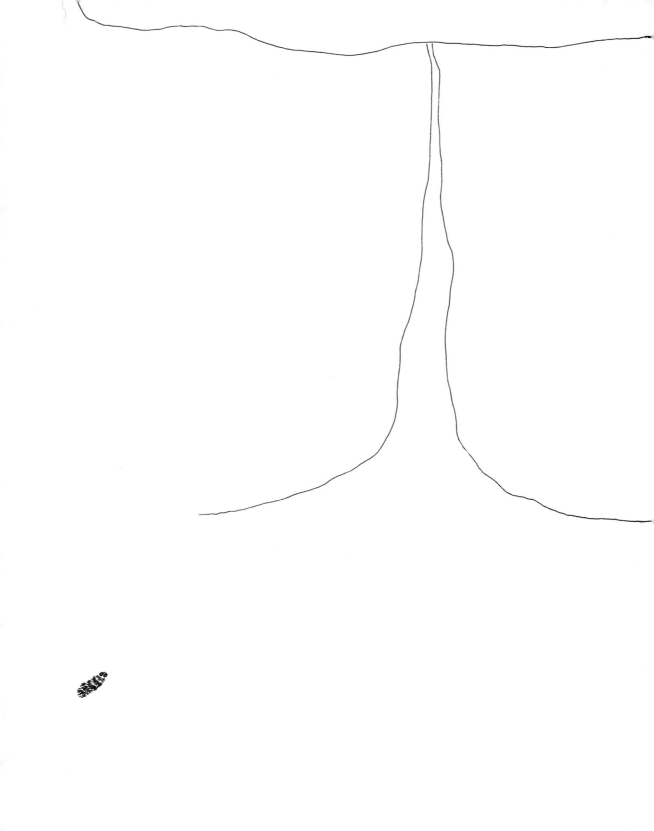

One day at the pillar, three thuds startled
Stripe. Three big caterpillars had
fallen from someplace and smashed.

Two seemed dead but one still wiggled.
Stripe whispered, "What happened?
Can I help?"

He made out just a few words.
"The top... they'll see...
butterflies alone..."

The caterpillar died.

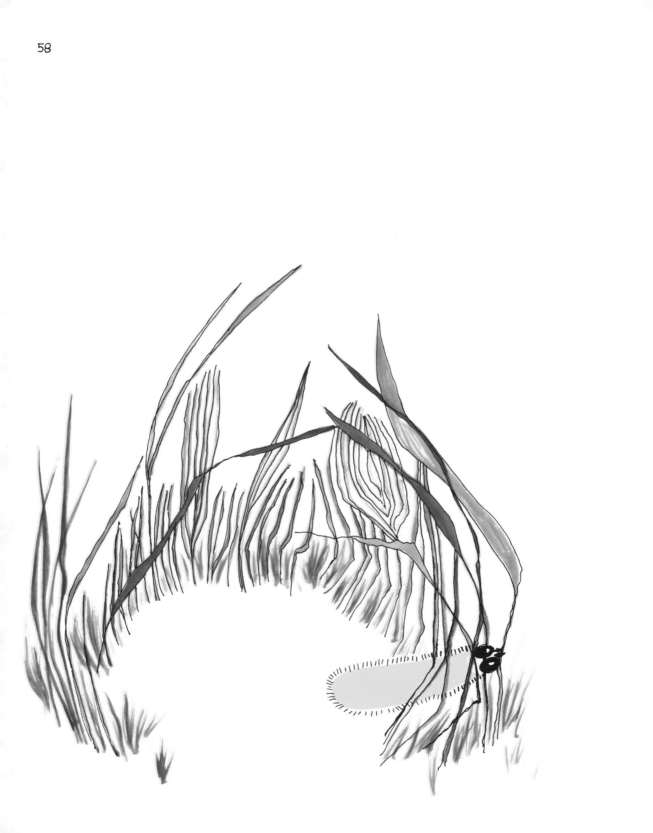

Stripe crawled home and told Yellow.

They were both very sober and quiet. What did the mysterious message mean?

Had the caterpillars fallen from the very top?

Finally Stripe announced:
"I've got to know. I must go and
find out the secret of the top."

And more gently,
"Will you come and help me?"

Yellow struggled inside.

She loved Stripe and wanted to be with him.
She wanted to help him succeed.

But — she just couldn't believe that the top was worth all it asks to get there.

She wanted to get "up" too; the crawling life wasn't enough for her either.

She also had to admit that it looked like the pile was the only way to do it.

Stripe seemed so sure that Yellow felt ashamed not to agree. She also felt stupid and embarrassed since she could never put her reasons into words that his kind of logic would accept.

Yet somehow, waiting and not being sure was better than action she couldn't believe in.

She couldn't explain, she couldn't
prove anything—but for all her
love she couldn't go with Stripe.

She just knew climbing was a wrong
way to get high.

"No," she said, heartsick.
And Stripe left her
for his climb.

CHAPTER IV

Yellow was desolate
without Stripe.

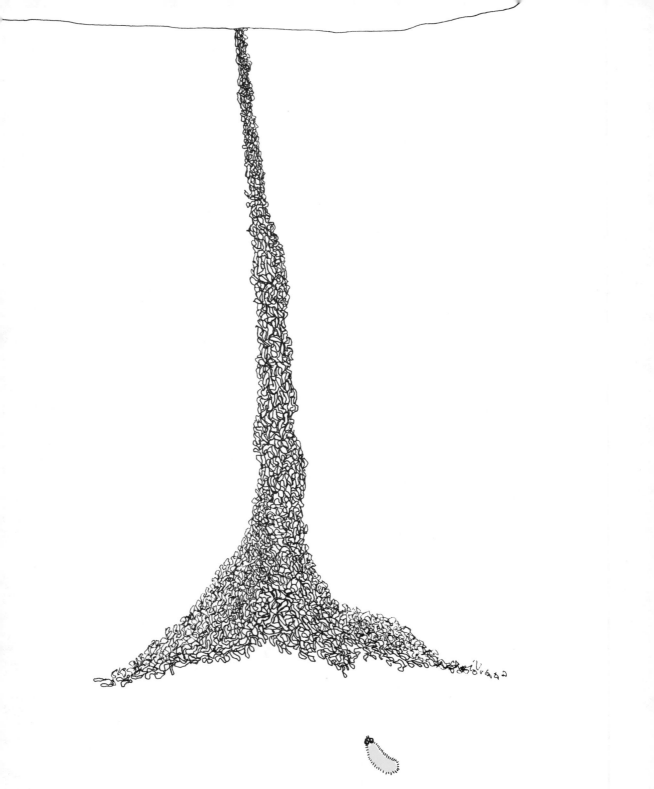

She crawled daily to the pile looking
for him and returned home at night sad,
but half relieved that she never saw
him. If she had, she feared she might
plunge after him knowing that she
shouldn't.

She felt like doing something, anything,
rather than this uncertain waiting.

"What in the world do I
really want?" she sighed.
"It seems different
every few minutes.
"But I know there must
be more."

Finally, she became numb and wandered
away from everything familiar.

One day a grey-haired
caterpillar hanging
upside down on a branch
surprised her.

He seemed caught in
some hairy stuff.

"You seem in trouble,"
she said. "Can I help?"

"No, my dear, I have to do this
to become a butterfly."

Her whole insides leapt.
"Butterfly – that word," she thought.
"Tell me, sir, what is a butterfly?"

"It's what you are meant to
become. It flies with beautiful
wings and joins the earth to
heaven. It drinks only nectar
from the flowers and carries
the seeds of love from one
flower to another."

" Without butterflies
the world would soon have few flowers."

"It can't be true!" gasped Yellow.
"How can I believe there's a
butterfly inside you or me, when
all I see is a fuzzy worm?"

"How does one become a butterfly?"
she asked pensively.

"You must want to fly so much
that you are willing to give
up being a caterpillar."

"You mean to die?" asked Yellow, remembering
the three who fell out of the sky.

"Yes and No," he answered.
"What <u>looks</u> like you will die
but what's <u>really</u> you will still
live. Life is changed, not
taken away. Isn't that
different from those who
die without ever becoming
butterflies?"

"And if I decide to become a butterfly,"
said Yellow hesitantly. "What do I do?"

"Watch me. I'm making a cocoon.

"It looks like I'm hiding, I know,
but a cocoon is no escape.

"It's an in-between house where
the change takes place.

"It's a big step since you can
never return to caterpillar life.

"During the change, it will seem
to you or to anyone who might
peek that nothing is happening —
but the butterfly is already
becoming.

"It just takes time!"

" And there's something else!

" Once you are a butterfly, you can <u>really</u> love - the kind of love that makes new life. It's better than all the hugging caterpillars can do."

"Oh, let me go and get Stripe," Yellow said. But she sadly knew he was too far into the pile to possibly reach.

"Don't be sad," said her new friend. "If you change, you can fly and show him how beautiful butterflies are. Maybe he will want to become one too!"

Yellow was torn in anguish:

"What if Stripe comes back and I'm not there? What if he doesn't recognize my new self? Suppose he decides to stay a caterpillar?

"At least we can do <u>something</u> as caterpillars— we can crawl and eat. We can love in <u>some</u> way. How can two cocoons get together at all? How awful to get stuck in a cocoon!"

How could she risk the only life she knew when it seemed so unlikely she could ever be a glorious winged creature?

What did she have to go on? — seeing another caterpillar who believed enough to make his own cocoon. — and that peculiar hope which had kept her off the pillar and leapt within her when she heard about butterflies.

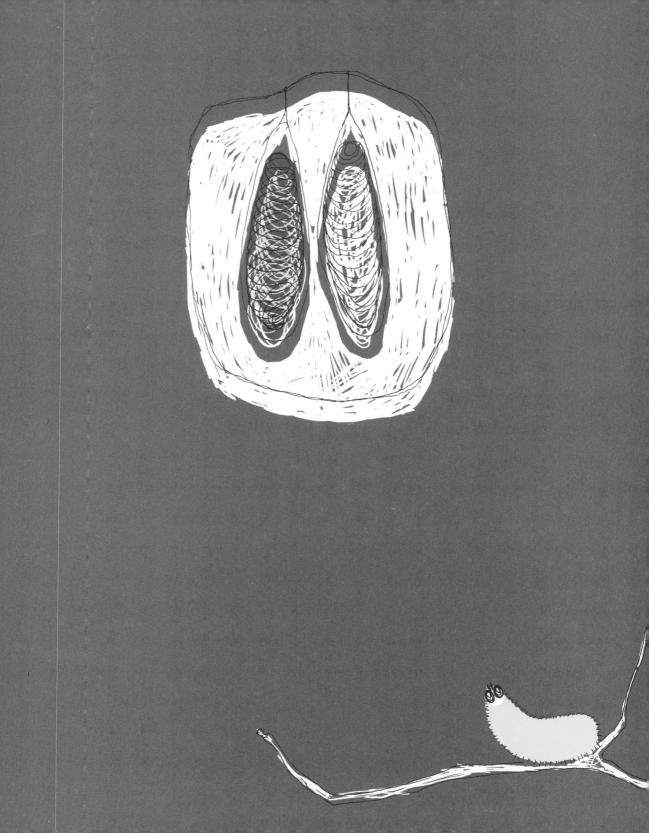

The grey-haired caterpillar
continued to cover himself
with silky threads. As he
wove the last bit around
his head he called:

"You'll be a beautiful butterfly —
we're all waiting for you!"

And Yellow decided to risk for a butterfly.

For courage she hung right beside the other cocoon and began to spin her own.

"Imagine, I didn't even know I could do this. That's some encouragement that I'm on the right track. If I have inside me the stuff to make cocoons — maybe the stuff of butterflies is there too."

CHAPTER V

Stripe made much faster progress this time. He was bigger and stronger since he had taken time out. From the beginning he determined to get to the top.

He especially avoided meeting the eyes of other crawlers. He knew how fatal such contact could be.

He tried not to think of Yellow.

He disciplined himself neither to feel nor to be distracted.

Stripe didn't seem just "disciplined" to others— he seemed ruthless. Even among climbers he was special.

He didn't think he was against anybody. He was just doing what he had to if he was to get to the top.

"Don't blame me if you don't succeed! It's a tough life. Just make up your mind," he would have said had any caterpillar complained.

Then one day he was near his goal.

Stripe had done well but when light finally filtered down from the top, he was close to exhaustion.

At this height there was almost no movement. All held their positions with every skill a lifetime of climbing had taught them. Every small move counted terribly.

There was no communication. Only the outsides touched. They were like cocoons to one another.

Then one day Stripe heard a crawler above him saying,

"None of us can get any higher without getting rid of _them_."

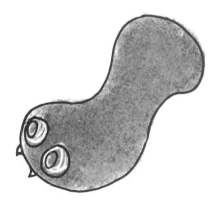

Soon after, he felt tremendous pressure and shaking. Then came screams and falling bodies. Then silence; lots more light and less weight from above.

Stripe felt awful with this new knowledge. The mystery of the pillar was clearing.

He now knew what had happened to the three caterpillars.

He now knew what must always happen on the pillar.

Frustration surged through Stripe. But as he was agreeing this was the only way "up" he heard a tiny whisper from the top:

"There's nothing here at all!"

It was answered by another:

"Quiet, fool! They'll hear you down the pillar. We're where _they_ want to get. That's what's here!"

Stripe felt frozen. To be so high and not high at all! It only looked good from the bottom.

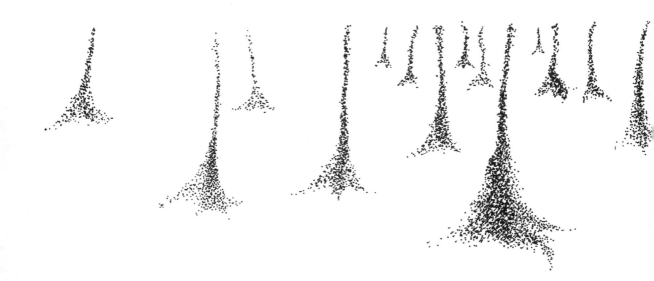

The whisper came again,
"Look over there – another pillar –
and there too – everywhere!"

Stripe became angry as well as frustrated.
"My pillar," he moaned, "only one of thousands.

"Millions of caterpillars climbing nowhere!

"Something is really wrong but. . .
what else is there?"

His life with Yellow seemed so far away.
That wasn't it either — not quite.
"Yellow!" He let her image fill his being.
"You knew something, didn't you? Was it <u>courage</u>
to wait?
"Maybe she was right. I wish I were with her."
"I could go down," he thought. "I'd look ridiculous
but maybe it's better than what's happening here."

But Stripe's thought was interrupted by bursts of movement all over his level. Each seemed to be making a last effort to find some entry to the top. But with every push the top layer tightened.

Finally one caterpillar gasped, "Unless we try together nobody will reach the top. Maybe if we give <u>one</u> big push! "They can't hold us down forever!"

But before they could act there were cries and commotion of another kind. Stripe struggled to the edge to see the cause.

A brilliant yellow winged creature was circling the pillar, moving freely — a wonderful sight! How did it get so high without climbing?

When Stripe poked out his head
the creature seemed to recognize
him. It extended its legs and
tried to grab him.

Stripe caught himself just
before being pulled out of the
pile. The brilliant creature
let go and looked sadly into
his eyes.

That look activated excitement
Stripe hadn't felt since he
first saw the pillar. Words
from the past returned,
". . . butterflies alone."

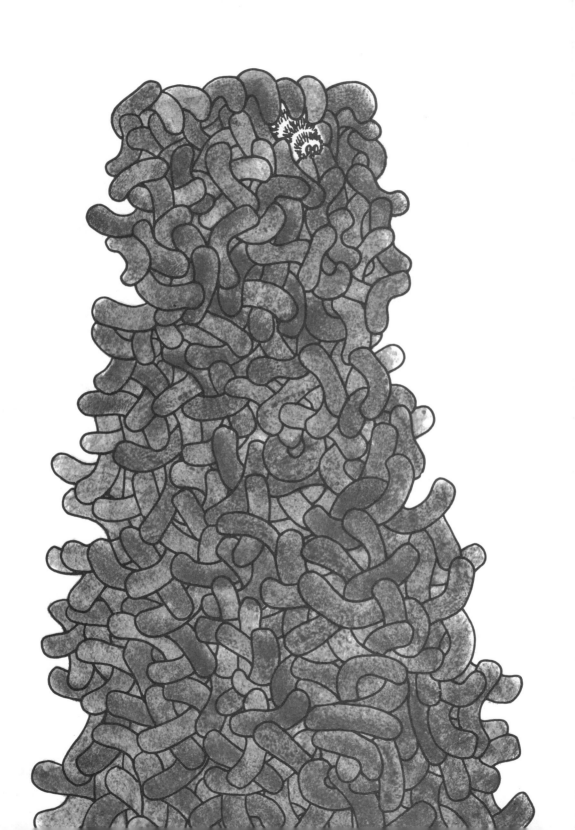

"Is <u>this</u> a butterfly?"

And what did it mean —
" the top... they'll see..." ?

It was all so strange and yet
like it was supposed to be.

And those eyes with the
look of Yellow.
Could it be...?

Such impossible thoughts!
Yet the excitement inside
wouldn't stop.

He grew happy.
Somehow he could escape,
he could be carried away.

But as this possibility became
real, something else grew
inside. He felt he shouldn't
escape like this.

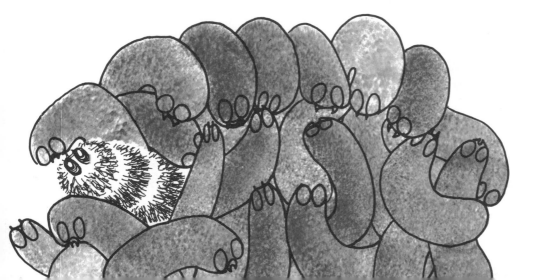

Looking into the creature's eyes
he could hardly bear the love he
saw there. He felt unworthy.
He wanted to change, to make
up for all the times he had
refused to look at the other.

He tried to tell her what
he felt.

He stopped struggling.
The others stared at him
as though he were mad.

CHAPTER VI

He turned around and began down the pillar. This time he didn't curl up. He stretched out full length and looked straight into the eyes of each caterpillar.

He marveled at the variety and beauty, amazed that he had never noticed it before.

He whispered to each, "I've been up; there's nothing there."

Most paid no attention; they were too intent on climbing.

One said, "It's sour grapes. He's bitter. I bet he never made it to the top."

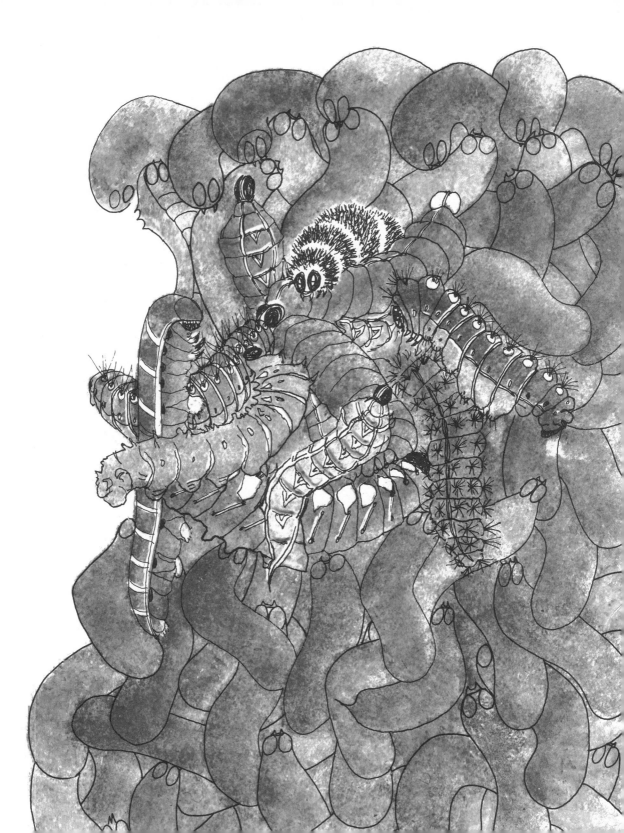

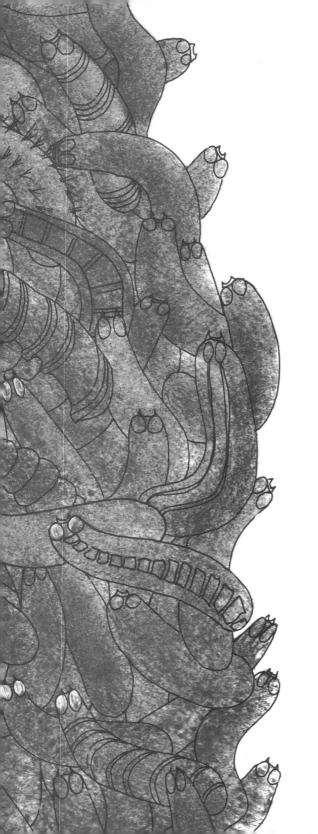

But some were shocked and even stopped climbing to hear him better.

One of these whispered in anquish, "Don't say it even if it's true. What else can we do?"

Stripe's answer shocked them all — including himself!

"We can <u>fly</u>!

"We can <u>become butterflies</u>!

"There's nothing at the top and <u>it doesn't matter</u>!"

As he heard his own message he realized how he had misread the instinct to get high. To get to the "top" he must fly, not climb.

Stripe looked at each caterpillar inebriated with joy that there could be a butterfly inside.

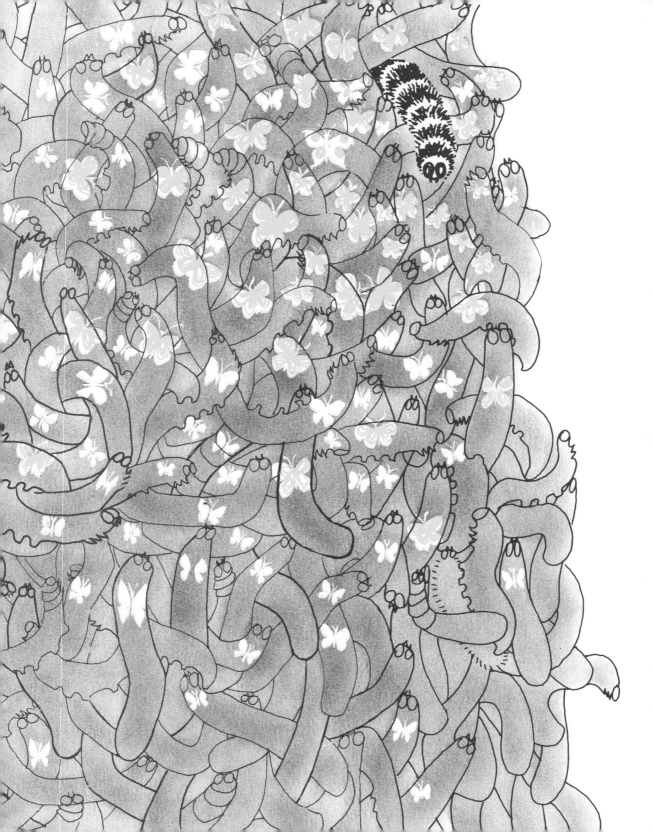

But the reaction was worse
than before. He saw fear in
eyes. They didn't stop to
listen or speak.

This happy, glorious news was
too much to take — too
good to be true.

And if it wasn't true?

The hope that lit up
the pillar dimmed. All
seemed confused and
unreal.

The way down was
so immensely long.

The vision of the
butterfly faded.

Doubt flooded Stripe.
The pile took on horrible dimensions.

He struggled on - barely - blindly.
It seemed wrong to give up
believing - yet believing seemed
impossible.

A crawler sneered, "How could
you swallow such a story? Our
life is earth and climbing. Look
at us worms! We couldn't be
butterflies inside. Make the best of
it and enjoy caterpillar living!"

"Perhaps he's right," sighed Stripe.
"I haven't any proof. Did I only
make it up because I needed
it so much?"

And in pain he continued
down searching for those
eyes which would let him
whisper,
   "I saw a butterfly—
      there can be more
      to life."

One day —
finally —
he was down.

CHAPTER VII

Tired and sad, Stripe
crawled off to the old place
where Yellow and he
had romped.

She was not there, and he
was too exhausted to go
further.

He curled up and fell asleep.

When he finally awoke he
found the yellow creature
fanning him with wings
of light.

"Is this a dream?"
he wondered.

But the dream creature acted
awfully real. She stroked him
with her feelers and most of all
looked at him so lovingly that
he began to trust that what he
had said about becoming a
butterfly might be true.

She walked a little distance
away, then flew back. She
repeated it as if he should
follow.

So he did.

130

They came to a
branch from which
hung two torn sacks.

The creature kept on
inserting her head,
then her tail,
into one of them.

Then she would fly to him
and touch him.

Her feelers quivered
and Stripe knew
she was speaking.

He couldn't make out words.

Then slowly he seemed
to understand. . . .

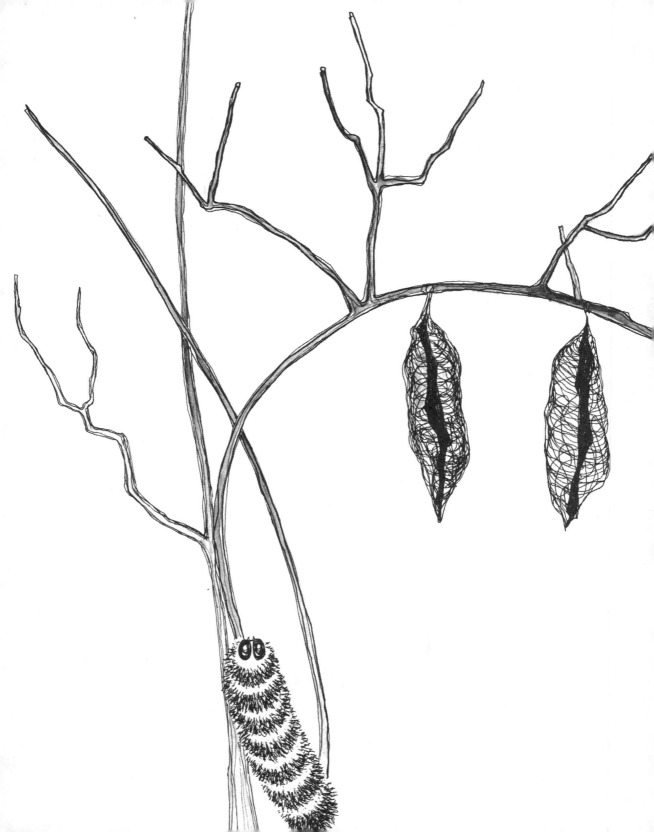

. . . Somehow he knew what to do.

Stripe climbed — again.

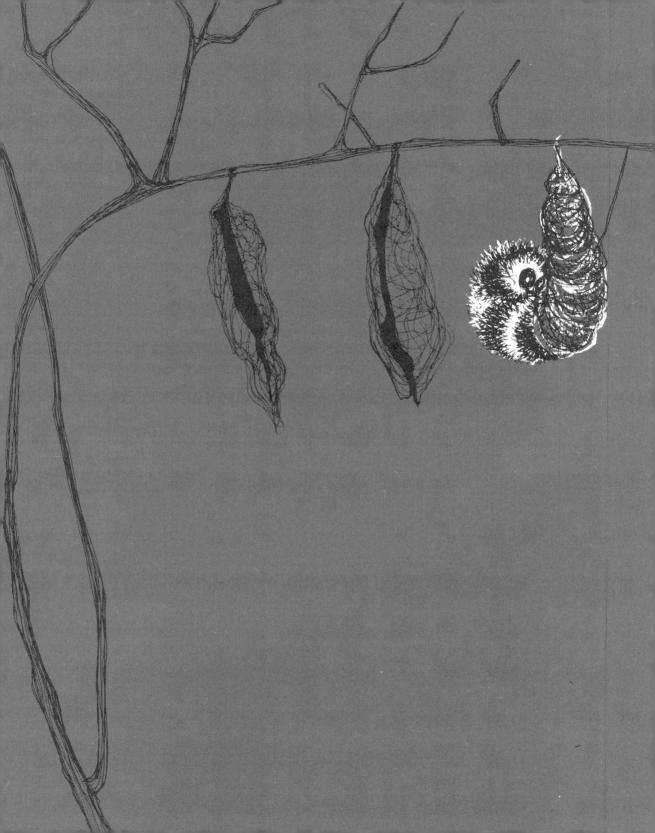

It got darker and darker
and he was afraid.

He felt he had
to let go of

everything. . . .

and Yellow waited . . . .

. . . until one day . . .

THE END . . . . .

. . . or the beginning

ACKNOWLEDGEMENTS

It takes a lot of butterflies to make a world full of flowers.
It takes a lot of people to make a book.

Someone asked an artist how long it took him to make a certain picture. "Five minutes and my whole lifetime," he responded. This book is like that.

I want to thank with all my heart each who has given either to the book itself or to the "lifetime" that made it possible.

For the "lifetime contributors" perhaps the book itself is the best thanks I can give. It was done for all I know and the millions I don't yet know but with whom I share the search for the "more" of life in a world of Peace with Justice.

I want to try to thank by name those who have helped the process of the book itself. I fear to forget someone but hope they will forgive and understand.

Advisors and encouragers: Carole Spearin McCauley, Carol Donahoe, Frances Finch, Theresa Beirs, Ann Hope, Carolyn Gratton, Veronica Forbes, Dorothy Rasenberger, Ann Burke, Janet Kalven, Victoria Jadez, Jeanne Heiberg. Thanks to all my friends in the Grail movement especially the Akhmim team, Grailville and the New York Grail Shop. Thanks to Edward Callanan, Edward Nemeth S.J., Father Alan Sprenger, Philip Hoelle S.M., Lynn + David Harbert, Virginia + Richard Baron, Pat + Gerry Mische, the Browns, Sheltzes, Lipscombs, Shudas, Gaspers, Wilsons, Kepes. Then there are the women of C.W.U. especially Claire Randall + Margaret Shannon, the U.P.W., + Y.W.C.A. Thanks to Cheryl, Mary, Irma, Velma, Emily, Eileen Egan, Kathy Silva, Sarah Cunningham, Ann Beneduce, Edris Eckhardt, the Abbey Press team, Haim Kandell, and my devil's advocate Emanuel. Special thanks to my mother who has sustained her care for the whole long time of writing and art.

Thanks to the public libraries in Hartford, East Orange and Albany.

To all at Paulist-Newman Press thanks, especially Richard Payne + John Kirvan, Urban, Joe, Helen, Sue, Mary, Vivian.

Color separations: G.T.O. Little Ferry N.J.: Emile Cohen, Lowell Cook.